A TRUE BOOK™

The Southwest

D0061821

DANA MEACHEN RAU

Children's Press®
An Imprint of Scholastic Inc.
New York Toronto London Auckland Sydney
Mexico City New Delhi Hong Kong
Danbury, Connecticut

Front cover, center: The Alamo in San Antonio, Texas
Front cover, top right: Golden Driller statue in Tulsa, Oklahoma
Font cover, bottom left: Balloons in the International Balloon Fiesta in Albuquerque, New Mexico

Content Consultant
James Wolfinger, PhD
Associate Professor
DePaul University
Chicago, Illinois

Library of Congress Cataloging-in-Publication Data

Rau, Dana Meachen, 1971–
  The Southwest/by Dana Meachen Rau.
      p. cm.—(A true book)
  Includes bibliographical references and index.
  ISBN-13: 978-0-531-24853-9 (lib. bdg.)   ISBN-10: 0-531-24853-4 (lib. bdg.)
  ISBN-13: 978-0-531-28328-8 (pbk.)   ISBN-10: 0-531-28328-3 (pbk.)
  1. Southwestern States—Juvenile literature. I. Title. II. Series.
  F785.7.R38 2012
  979—dc23   2011031705

All rights reserved. Published in 2012 by Children's Press, an imprint of Scholastic Inc.
Printed in China 62
SCHOLASTIC, CHILDREN'S PRESS, A TRUE BOOK, and associated logos are trademarks and/or registered trademarks of Scholastic Inc.
1 2 3 4 5 6 7 8 9 10 R 21 20 19 18 17 16 15 14 13 12

Find the Truth!

Everything you are about to read is true **except** for one of the sentences on this page.

Which one is **TRUE**?

T or F   Santa Fe, New Mexico, was established more than 400 years ago.

T or F   "Black gold" is a name for coal.

Find the answers in this book.

3

Contents

THE **BIG** TRUTH!

Animals of the Southwest

Roadrunner

Johnson Space Center

Georgia O'Keeffe often painted pictures of rocks and skulls she found in the deserts of New Mexico.

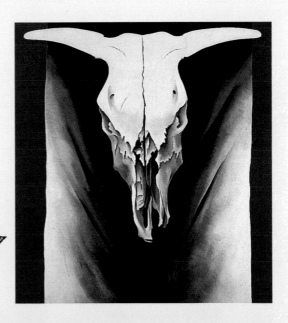

N
W   E
S

LEGEND
⊗ State capitals
● Major cities

G R E A T

Missouri River

R O C K Y   M O U N T A I N S

The United States

0   miles   200
0   km   200

Colorado River

P L A I N S

⊗ Santa Fe
● Albuquerque

⊗ Oklahoma City

OKLAHOMA

ARIZONA

Red River

⊗ Phoenix

NEW MEXICO

Carlsbad
Caverns

Fort Worth ● ● Dallas

Sonoran
Desert

● Tucson

● El Paso

TEXAS

Rio Grande

Austin ⊗

Houston
●

● San Antonio

M E X I C O

Gulf of
Mexico

6

Cactus and Canyon Country

The Southwest region of the United States is made up of four states. The states are Arizona, New Mexico, Oklahoma, and Texas. To the south of the region is Mexico. To the east is the Texas coastline along the Gulf of Mexico. The western edge of the region is formed by the Colorado River in Arizona.

 Texas is the only southwestern state with a coastline.

Look at the Land

The Southwest includes different **landforms**. The Great Plains are vast grasslands that reach across Oklahoma into Texas and New Mexico. The grasslands are perfect for huge cattle ranches because they provide plenty of grass to feed large herds of cows or livestock. Other parts of the plains are wet enough to support farms.

Millions of bison roamed the vast southwestern grasslands until overhunting almost killed them off.

Nearly 4.5 million people visit the Grand Canyon every year.

Much of the Southwest is covered in rocky deserts, high **plateaus**, and rugged mountains. The Rocky Mountains reach into northern New Mexico. The Colorado River cuts into Arizona in the state's northwest corner. Over millions of years, the Colorado has carved a path through the rock of the plateau. This created the Grand Canyon. The canyon extends for more than 200 miles (322 kilometers). In some parts, it is 1 mile (1.6 km) deep.

Animals seek out what little shade they can find in the hot desert.

Plants such as yuccas have adapted to survive in New Mexico's dry deserts.

Climate

The Southwest is known for its hot temperatures. But beyond the heat, the **climate** varies across the region. Parts of the east are humid, including Oklahoma and eastern Texas. Summers are hot and winters are cool. As you move west, the climate changes to semiarid. These areas have clear skies, dry air, and very little rain. Eastern Arizona, southern New Mexico, and parts of Texas are arid—the driest desert climate.

Hot and Dry

Most of the Southwest is very dry. There is not much rainfall. Cacti are common. These plants have thick skin that stores water for use in dry periods. Humans must also adapt to the small amounts of rain. Farmers use **irrigation** to bring water to their crops. In the driest areas, such as the Sonoma Desert in Arizona, farming is very difficult.

Cacti do not need much water to survive.

Summer is the driest time of year. Plants dry out. They can catch fire in the heat. The fire quickly spreads and becomes a wildfire. Wildfires can destroy people's homes and cost lives. But wildfires also help keep the **ecosystem** healthy. They clear out dead plants and help certain plants release their seeds.

The summer heat can be intense. But a hot climate can be good. Winters stay quite warm. Many people visit the region during the winter for this reason.

Wildfires often burn for weeks and can damage hundreds of square miles.

Tornadoes can quickly destroy homes and businesses.

Oklahoma and Texas are part of Tornado Alley, the area of the United States where tornadoes hit most.

A Dangerous Combination

Oklahoma and Texas are caught between climates. Eastern parts of these states enjoy warm, moist air blowing in from the Gulf. But hot, dry air also moves in from the arid and semiarid west. Cooler air from the north is added to the mix. This combination can be disastrous. Blizzards and heavy thunderstorms can develop. So can tornadoes. These violent storms often cause serious damage and loss of life.

Native Americans of the Southwest planted crops such as corn and beans.

14

CHAPTER 2

History of the Southwest

For thousands of years, the Southwest was home to many Native American groups. The land was as dry then as it is now. But the native groups grew crops. They built irrigation systems to bring water from nearby rivers to their crops. This same technique is in use today.

Many Native Americans used the soil of the region to make homes out of **adobe** bricks. Some of these **pueblos** stood many stories high, and many still stand today.

Spanish Settlers

In the 1500s, Spanish soldiers came to the Americas in search of gold and treasure. One of these explorers was Francisco Vásquez de Coronado. Coronado set out from Mexico City to the present-day Southwest in 1540.

More people followed. The Spanish set up **missions** to teach native groups their religion. They forced Native Americans to work for them. Battles between settlers and native groups were common.

Southwestern Timeline

1540
Francisco Vásquez de Coronado explores the Southwest.

1821
Mexico gains independence from Spain.

By the mid-1600s, Spain controlled a large territory it called New Spain. New Spain covered Central America and a large part of the current southern United States. Spanish villages had sprung up across the region by the end of the 1700s.

The people of Mexico wanted **independence** from Spain. In 1821, they fought for and won their freedom. At this time, Mexico included the present-day states of Texas, New Mexico, Arizona, and parts of Oklahoma.

1838–1839

Native Americans travel the Trail of Tears into Indian Territory.

1846–1848

Mexico and the United States fight the Mexican-American War over ownership of land.

1836

Texas gains independence from Mexico.

American Settlers

People in the United States were eager to explore lands west of the Appalachian Mountains and Mississippi River. The Mexican government wanted more settlers in their large territory. They hoped this would help develop the land and bring more money into the country. With this in mind, the Mexican government allowed Americans to settle there. But they had to obey Mexico's laws.

Many Americans began moving westward in the 1800s.

The United States gained more than 500,000 square miles (1 million sq km) of land in the Mexican-American War.

The Mexican-American War allowed the United States to continue expanding west.

Arguments broke out between American settlers and the Mexican government. Texas wanted to govern itself. After many battles, Texas became independent in 1836. More American settlers came to the area. So did **immigrants** from Europe.

Texas became a U.S. state in 1845. But the U.S. and Mexican governments argued over Texas's borders. This led to the Mexican-American War (1846–1848). The United States won, gaining more territory in the west. Parts of this territory became the states of New Mexico and Arizona in 1912.

Indian Territory

Not everyone moved west by choice. Southeastern states forced resident Native Americans to move to Indian Territory. This was land the United States set aside for them in present-day Oklahoma. Most made the trip in the 1830s. Their journey is called the Trail of Tears because many died.

The United States later took away some of Indian Territory. In 1889, the U.S. government set up a race for American settlers to claim land in the area. White settlers soon outnumbered Native Americans and Oklahoma became a state in 1907.

Around 15,000 Native Americans died on the Trail of Tears.

Artists and Inventors of the Southwest

Woody Guthrie

Woody Guthrie (1912–1967) (left) was a folk singer who wrote songs about America, including "This Land Is Your Land." He was born in Oklahoma.

Steven Spielberg (1946–) is a film director whose work includes *Jurassic Park* and *E.T.: The Extra-Terrestrial*. He grew up in Arizona.

Gene Roddenberry (1921–1991) was a television writer and producer. His most popular creation is *Star Trek*. He was born in Texas.

Georgia O'Keeffe (1887–1986) was an artist whose paintings captured the colors of the Southwest landscape. She spent much of her life in New Mexico.

Cowboys are still a big part of southwestern culture.

CHAPTER 3

People of the Southwest

Spanish explorers first brought horses and cattle to the Southwest in the 1600s. Settlers and natives worked as America's first cowboys, using the horses to herd the cattle. By the late 1800s, the Southwest needed lots of cowboys. They worked the region's growing ranches. They took cattle on long rides across the prairie to market.

This history has influenced much of southwestern culture today. Spanish, Mexican, native, and cowboy traditions appear everywhere in clothing, food, architecture, and festivities.

Many Mexican-Americans live in the Southwest.

Spanish and Mexican Traditions

The region's history is still a part of everyday life in the Southwest. Celebrations, architecture, food, and names reflect Spanish and Mexican traditions. New Mexico and Texas have two of the largest Hispanic populations in the United States. Some of these people are related to the settlers of long ago. Others are immigrants who have come from nearby Mexico more recently. Many southwesterners speak both English and Spanish.

Native Americans Today

The Southwest has a large Native American population. The largest groups include the Navajo, the Pueblo, and the Cherokee. There are many other groups as well. Crafts such as weaving, pottery, and jewelry are one way these groups connect to their long history. Some Native American schools teach their native language to young students so that it is not forgotten.

Many Native Americans continue to practice the arts and crafts of their ancestors.

Old Traditions, Modern Places

Santa Fe, New Mexico, was founded in 1609. It is one of the region's oldest cities. People today celebrate its long history. A festival held each year remembers a peaceful end to fighting between native Pueblo and Spanish settlers. Actors reenact the return of the town's settlers in 1692.

The Oklahoma State Fair is held in Oklahoma City every summer. Millions of people visit. Residents get the chance to show off the best of their culture and economy from music and food to rodeo competitions and displays of prize livestock.

Santa Fe features many buildings inspired by those of the Pueblo people who once lived in the area.

Houston's underground tunnel stretches across 95 city blocks.

Houston is the fourth-largest city in the United States.

Keeping Cool in the Big City

Most southwesterners live in or near cities. Houston, Texas, is the region's largest city. Skyscrapers rise above the ground. But Houston also extends below the streets. Engineers built an air-conditioned underground tunnel filled with restaurants and shops. People enter the tunnel to escape the summer heat.

Arizona cities such as Tucson also provide a way to keep cool. Splash pads are free in public playgrounds. Visitors play in fountains to have fun and cool off.

Animals of the Southwest

Many animals make their homes in the rugged land of the Southwest.

Many types of rattlesnakes live in the Southwest. Rattlesnakes shake the rattles on their tails to warn enemies to stay away. Rattlesnakes are good hunters, with sharp, poisonous fangs.

Armadillos have fur like most mammals. But they also have a hard shell. This tough covering helps protect them from enemies. Their strong claws help them dig in the dirt.

Greater roadrunners live in open deserts. They can run up to 18 miles (29 km) per hour. Roadrunners eat small birds and mammals, insects, snakes, and lizards.

Oil is important to the southwestern economy.

CHAPTER 4

Resources and Economy

The people of the Southwest make an income through a variety of jobs. Some people work in factories that produce chemicals, computers, or electronics. Other people work in hotels or restaurants, helping those who are visiting the area. Some people do research. They might develop new technology or study the region's history. But the Southwest is probably best known for two very specific products: oil and cattle.

Early oil drills were powered by steam engines.

Petrochemical plants are a common sight in some parts of Texas.

Oil

Oil is so valuable that many people call it "black gold." People have developed many uses for oil. Its main use is to fuel cars, planes, and other vehicles. But some oil is turned into **petrochemicals**. These chemicals are used in plastics, makeup, paint, food, and medications. Many chemical products are made in factories in the Southwest. They are **exported** to other regions and countries. Factories employ thousands of workers and bring money into the region.

The discovery of major oil resources in 1901 allowed the population and economies of Texas and Oklahoma to grow. Tulsa, Oklahoma even built a statue celebrating oil called the Golden Driller.

However, oil is a limited resource. It is becoming harder to find and more expensive. Many people are working to limit oil use. Some support laws requiring cars to use less fuel. Other people are researching new fuels to replace oil.

The Spindletop oil field was one of the first major oil discoveries in Texas.

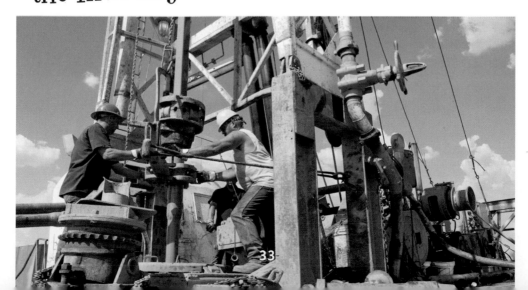

Ranching

Beef cattle are the Southwest's most important farm product. The grasslands that ranches depend on usually do fine in the region's arid climate. But sometimes the weather is worse than usual. In summer 2011, the region experienced one of its worst droughts in recorded history. Water and grasses disappeared. Cattle herds faced starvation. Many ranchers had to sell their cattle as quickly as possible. With so much cattle being sold at once, prices dropped. Ranchers may have lost more than $1 billion in the drought.

Cattle ranches are common in western Texas.

Less than an inch of rain fell on parts of Texas between September 2010 and July 2011.

Johnson Space Center is home to a control center where NASA officials monitor the progress of space missions.

Industries

The aerospace industry is important to the Southwest. It is particularly important in Texas. The Johnson Space Center was built in Houston in 1962. Astronauts still train there. After the space center was built, more aerospace businesses came to the state. Factories and research facilities employ thousands of people to build and invent new aircraft and engines. Companies develop food and other products for astronauts.

The Alamo was the site of an 1836 battle between Texas and Mexico.

Tourism is another important industry. Many people visit the Southwest to see places such as the Grand Canyon, the Alamo, and Carlsbad Caverns. They also visit Albuquerque, New Mexico, each year to watch the International Balloon Fiesta. Tourists eat and stay in the area. This brings money to local businesses. It also provides residents with jobs in hotels and restaurants.

Riding and Roping at a Rodeo

Rodeos began with cowboys competing with each other to show off who was best at riding horses and roping cattle. The first official rodeo contest with tickets and prizes was held in Arizona in 1888.

At a rodeo, cowboys and cowgirls compete in many events. They might have to rope a calf or wrestle a steer. They might be timed to see who can stay on a bucking horse or bull the longest.

Homes in Phoenix and other desert cities are built with adobe. Adobe keeps homes cool during the day and warm at night.

CHAPTER 5

A Growing Population

The Southwest is one of the driest areas of the United States. Yet the region's population has grown over the last 10 years. In fact, the Southwest had one of the largest population growths in the United States. This is according to the 2010 U.S. census. Many Americans move there to work or retire.

Adobe bricks are made from local mud and other materials, such as straw.

The Need for Water

One of the challenges of living in the Southwest is providing enough water for so many people. Southwesterners need to change the land to meet their needs.

People build dams to create bodies of usable water. The water running through the dams can help create electrical power. The water can be used to irrigate fields for growing crops.

The Hoover Dam on the Colorado River provides energy to several western and southwestern states.

The Central Arizona Project canal is 336 miles (540 km) long.

The Central Arizona Project brings water to dry areas.

Using the Colorado River

Canals are another method for bringing water to the people of the Southwest. The ancient Hohokam Indians of Arizona were the first to build a system of canals. The canals helped bring water from nearby rivers to their land. Today, Arizona uses a similar system.

In 1968, the Central Arizona Project began. Construction lasted 25 years. The project brought water from the Colorado River to Arizona's major cities through pumps and canals.

The Southwest's rock formations are red because they contain iron.

As more people move to the area, they will have to deal with the challenges of a land with very little water. But the land also has a lot to offer. Mild winters, clear skies, and beautiful scenery will always draw people to the Southwest. ★

True Statistics

Number of states in the region: 4

Major rivers of the region: Rio Grande, Red, Colorado

Major mountain ranges of the region: Rocky Mountains

Climate: Humid subtropical, semiarid, arid

Largest cities: Houston, TX; Phoenix, AZ; San Antonio, TX

Products: Oil, natural gas, copper, wheat, livestock

Borders of the region:

North: West and Midwest regions

East: Southeast region and the Gulf of Mexico

South: Mexico and the Gulf of Mexico

West: California and Nevada

Did you find the truth?

(T) Santa Fe, New Mexico, was established more than 400 years ago.

(F) "Black gold" is a name for coal.

Resources

Books

Augustin, Byron, and Jake Kubena. *The Grand Canyon*. New York: Marshall Cavendish Benchmark, 2010.

Gilpin, Daniel. *The Colorado River*. Milwaukee, WI: Gareth Stevens Publishing, 2004.

Kent, Deborah. *The Trail of Tears*. New York: Children's Press, 2005.

Lilly, Alexandra. *Spanish Colonies in America*. Minneapolis, MN: Compass Point Books, 2009.

Maynard, Charles W. *The Rocky Mountains*. New York: PowerKids Press, 2004.

McGowen, Tom. *The Alamo*. New York: Children's Press, 2003.

Miller, Millie, and Cyndi Nelson. *The United States of America: A State-by-State Guide*. New York: Scholastic Reference, 1999.

Rau, Dana Meachen. *North America*. Chanhassen, MN: The Child's World, 2004.

St. Lawrence, Genevieve. *The Pueblo and Their History*. Minneapolis, MN: Compass Point Books, 2006.

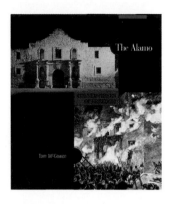

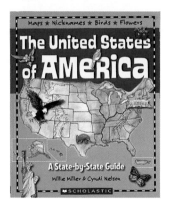

Web Sites

Smithsonian National Museum of American History

http://americanhistory.si.edu

Check out this site to see exhibits and learn about the growth of America.

U.S. Census 2010 Interactive Population Map

http://2010.census.gov/2010census/popmap

Learn about the populations of the states with this interactive map.

Places to Visit

The Alamo

300 Alamo Plaza
San Antonio, TX 78205
(210) 225-1391
www.thealamo.org
Visit the site of a famous battle as Texas fought for independence in 1836.

National Geographic Grand Canyon Visitor Center

450 State Route 64
Grand Canyon, AZ 86023
(928) 638-2468
http://explorethecanyon.com
Stop here before you enter the south rim of the Grand Canyon National Park to see films, shows, and get information about this amazing natural wonder.

 Visit this Scholastic web site for more information on the U.S. Southwest:
www.factsfornow.scholastic.com

Important Words

adobe (uh-DOH-bee) — bricks made of clay mixed with straw and dried in the sun

climate (KLYE-mit) — the usual weather in a place

ecosystem (EE-koh-sis-tuhm) — a community of animals and plants interacting with their environment

exported (EKS-port-id) — sent products to another country or region to be sold there

immigrants (IM-i-gruhntz) — people who come from abroad to live permanently in a country

independence (in-di-PEN-duhns) — freedom from the control of other people or things

irrigation (ir-i-GEY-shuhn) — the process of supplying water to crops by artificial means

landforms (LAND-formz) — natural features of the land

missions (MISH-uhnz) — churches established to share religion with native people

petrochemicals (pet-roh-KEM-ik-uhlz) — chemicals made from petroleum, or oil

plateaus (pla-TOHZ) — areas of high, flat land

pueblos (PWEB-lohz) — villages consisting of stone and adobe buildings built next to and on top of each other

Index

Page numbers in **bold** indicate illustrations

About the Author

Dana Meachen Rau is the author of more than 300 books for children. A graduate of Trinity College in Hartford, Connecticut, she has written fiction and nonfiction titles including early readers and books on science, history, cooking, and many other topics that interest her. She especially loves to write books that take her to other places, even when she doesn't have time for a vacation. Dana lives with her family in Burlington, Connecticut. To learn more about her books, please visit *www.danameachenrau.com*.